The Clown of Aleppo

Text Copyright© Luis Rodriguez

Illustrations Copyright© Leonardo Ariel Ariza Ardila

Library of Congress Cataloging-in-Publication Data

Summary: A courageous young Syrian dedicates and sacrifices his life for the children of his country and becomes an inspiration to the world.

ISBN: 978-0-9975433-3-9

Dedicated to Anas Al Basha's family, the people of Syria, my wife, Iolani, Teyo, and the rest of my family.

Luis Rodriguez

HERE IS A STORY THAT IS INSPIRING AND TRAGIC.

IT IS ABOUT A SUFFERING COUNTRY AND
SOME MAGIC.

IT BEGINS IN SYRIA WITH A HISTORY
THAT IS QUITE GRAND.

SINCE THE 8TH CENTURY MANY PEOPLE
HAVE WALKED THIS LAND.

ONCE HOME TO ONE OF THE MOST ANCIENT
CIVILIZATIONS ON EARTH,

AND AS PART OF THE FERTILE CRESCENT,
TO MANY EMPIRES IT GAVE BIRTH.

RULED BY THE SUMERIANS, ASSYRIANS, BABYLONIANS, AND THE PERSIANS;

ALEXANDER THE GREAT AND THE ROMANS ALSO LED THEIR OWN HISTORICAL EXCURSIONS.

IT WAS THE CENTER OF THE NEOLITHIC CULTURE FROM 10,000 BC.

TODAY MANY ANCIENT RUINS ARE DREADFULLY BEING TURNED INTO DEBRIS.

NOW LET US MEET ANAS AL BASHA.
THROUGH THE STREETS OF ALEPPO THIS BRAVE
SOUL DANCED AND SUNG;
WITH A HUMBLE COSTUME AND A HEART 24 YEARS
YOUNG.

HIS HOME INCLUDED A GREAT MOSQUE,
MEDIEVAL CITADEL, 2 MILLION PEOPLE, AND A SOUK.

A ONCE BUSTLING CITY, LIKE MANY OTHERS
IN SYRIA, AN AWFUL WAR TOOK.

A SPACE FOR HOPE WAS THE PLACE
ANAS AL BASHA SET HIS QUEST,

TO HELP HUNDREDS OF ORPHANED
CHILDREN LEFT HUNGRY AND DEPRESSED.

HE WOULD ACT OUT SKITS TO BRING
THESE BROKEN CHILDREN TOGETHER TO HEAL.

SO MANY WOULD WATCH IN AWE
WITH DISBELIEF THAT ANAS WAS REAL

250,000 INNOCENT PEOPLE
TRAPPED IN A WAR ZONE.

LITTLE INTERNATIONAL SUPPORT
MADE THEM FEEL AWFUL AND ALONE.

FOUR AND A HALF YEARS OF BRUTAL
CIVIL WAR—YET EACH DAY,

ANAS AL BASHA WOKE WITH BEAUTIFUL
THINGS TO SAY.

THE CLOWN OF ALEPPO USED LAUGHTER
TO SHINE LIGHT,
ON THE DARKNESS OF HIS PEOPLE'S
HORRIBLE PLIGHT.

HE SENT HIS PARENTS MONEY, THOUGH
LITTLE HE EARNED.

FOR THEIR SON'S PROTECTION,
THEIR PRAYERS YEARNED.

WITH HIS CHARM AND WORDS, BUBBLES
OF JOY HE WOULD MAKE,

GIVING THE CHILDREN'S PAIN A
MUCH-NEEDED BREAK.

THROUGH THE RUBBLE AND THROUGH THE TEARS,

THE CLOWN OF ALEPPO WOULD MELT EVERYONE'S FEARS.

DESPITE ALL THE DANGER, HE NEVER DID RECOIL.

INSTEAD, TO HIS MISSION, HE REMAINED LOYAL.

HE WAS WILLING TO FACE DEATH TO GIVE
THE CHILDREN HOPE.

WITH HIM GONE IT IS TIME TO COME
TOGETHER AND COPE.

AS WE HONOR ANAS AL BASHA'S MEMORY OF SACRIFICE AND DEDICATION;

WE ADD TO THE DREAM THAT SYRIA WILL ONE DAY GIVE ITS CHILDREN A PEACEFUL NATION.

LET US SHARE HIS STORY SO HIS SPIRIT MAY FOREVER BE AN INSPIRATION.

Be the hero of your life story.

A portion of the proceeds from
this book will be donated to
Anas Al Basha's Family.

Some of the many websites to donate and get involved to help Syria and its refugees.

HTTPS://WWW.CROWDRISE.COM/DONATE/PROJECT/US-FUND-FOR-UNICEF1

HTTPS://DONATE.WORLDVISION.ORG/SYRIAN-REFUGEE-CRISIS-1/

HTTPS://DONATE.DOCTORSWITHOUTBORDERS.ORG

HTTPS://PEOPLESMILLION.WHITEHELMETS.ORG/DONATE/PEOPLES-MILLION

The Clown
of Aleppo

Color Me

Color Me

Color Me

Color Me

Color Me

Be

The

Change

You wish to see in the world.

Thanks for your support

www.ingramcontent.com/pod-product-compliance
Lightning Source LLC
Chambersburg PA
CBHW042131080426
42735CB00001B/48